WARNINGS:

SUITABLE FOR AGES 12 AND UP AND ASK PARENTS FOR HELP TO ARRIVE AT THE AMOUNT IF NEEDED. DO NOT RUMMAGE THROUGH YOUR PARENTS' PURSE/WALLET!

IF YOU ARE OVER THE AGE OF 18 THEN CHILL BRO. HAVE FUN AND SAVE LIKE CRAZY TO REACH YOUR GOALS: WHETHER IT'S TO PAY FOR YOUR STUDIES OR TO TAKE A NICE VACATION!

WHAT IS YOUR GOAL?

_____

_____

_____

SAVE 30$ IN ONE MONTH

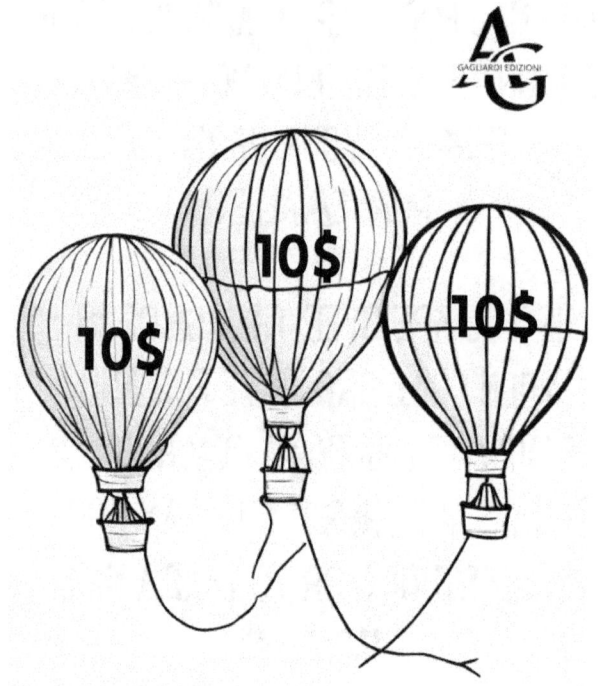

COLOR THE FIGURES EVERY TIME YOU HAVE STORED/OBTAINED THE AMOUNT!

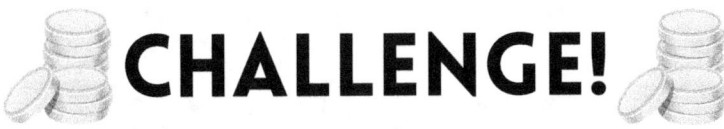

CHALLENGE!

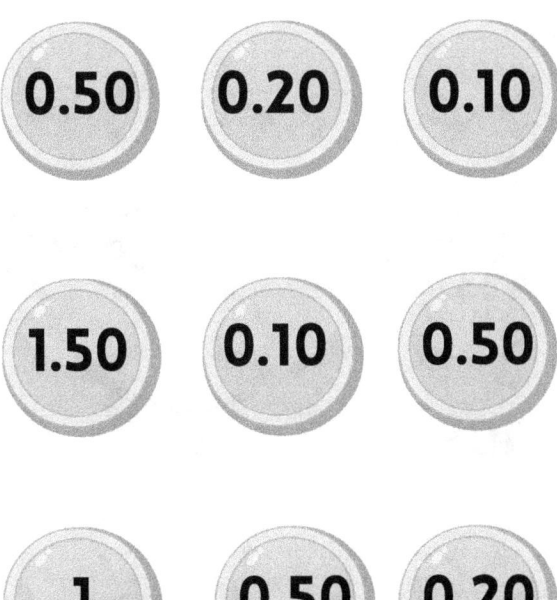

- HOW MUCH MONEY WILL YOU BE ABLE TO GET IN 2 DAYS? WRITE THE AMOUNT BELOW AND MARK WITH X!

_____

SAVE 40$ IN ONE MONTH

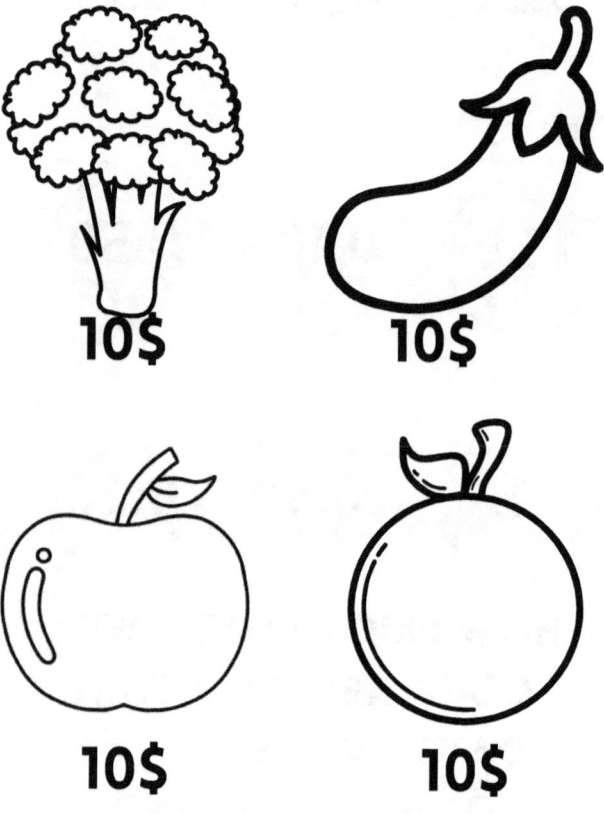

60$ IN ONE MONTH

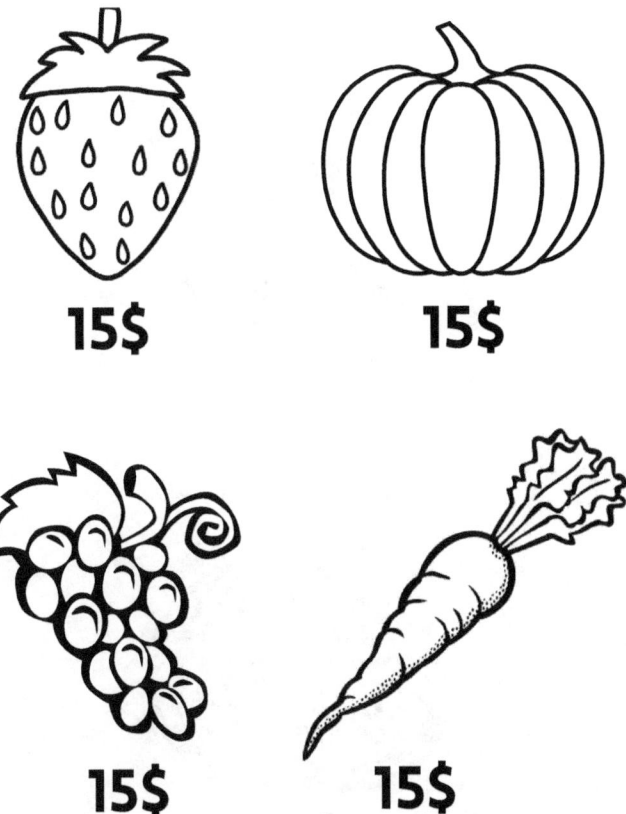

15$ 15$

15$ 15$

30$ IN ONE MONTH

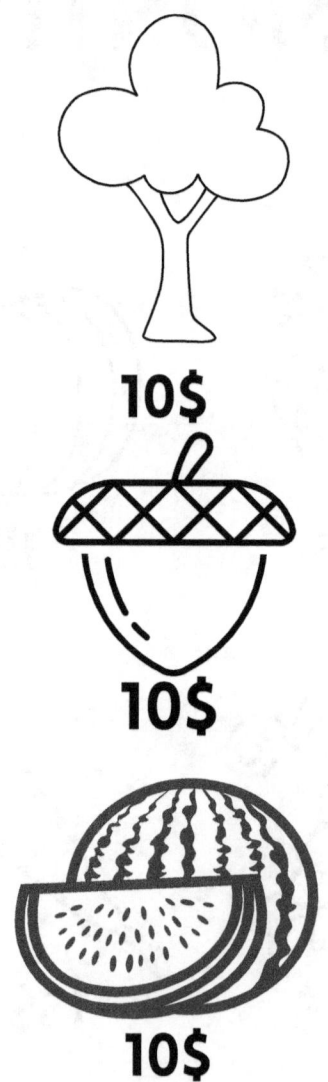

60$ IN ONE MONTH

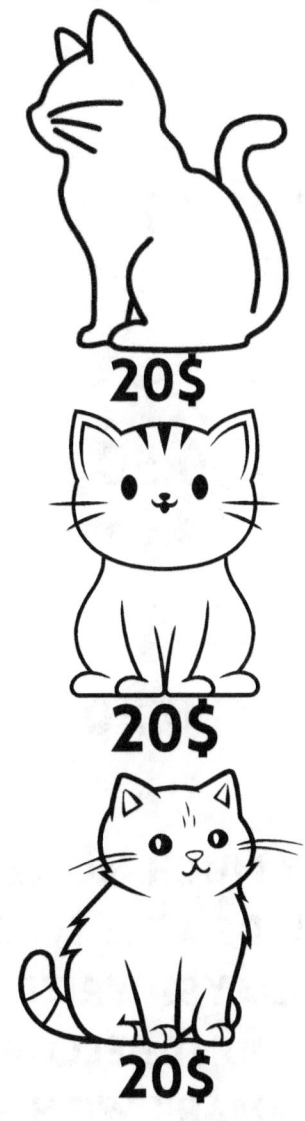

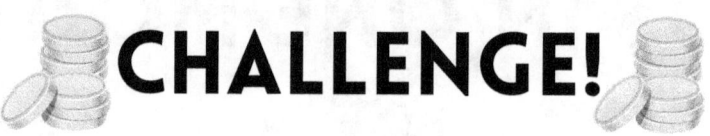 CHALLENGE!

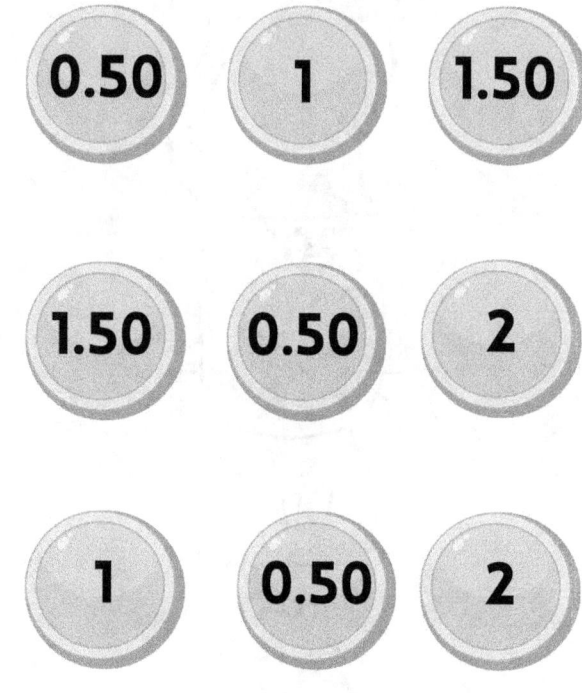

- HOW MUCH MONEY WILL YOU BE ABLE TO GET IN 3 DAYS? WRITE THE AMOUNT BELOW AND MARK WITH X

_____

60$ IN ONE MONTH

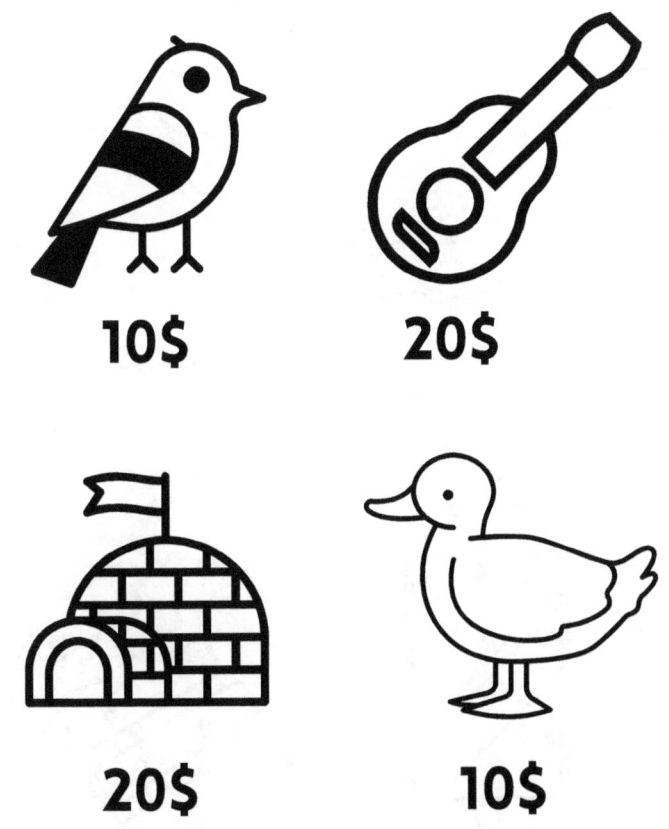

10$ 20$

20$ 10$

50$ IN ONE MONTH

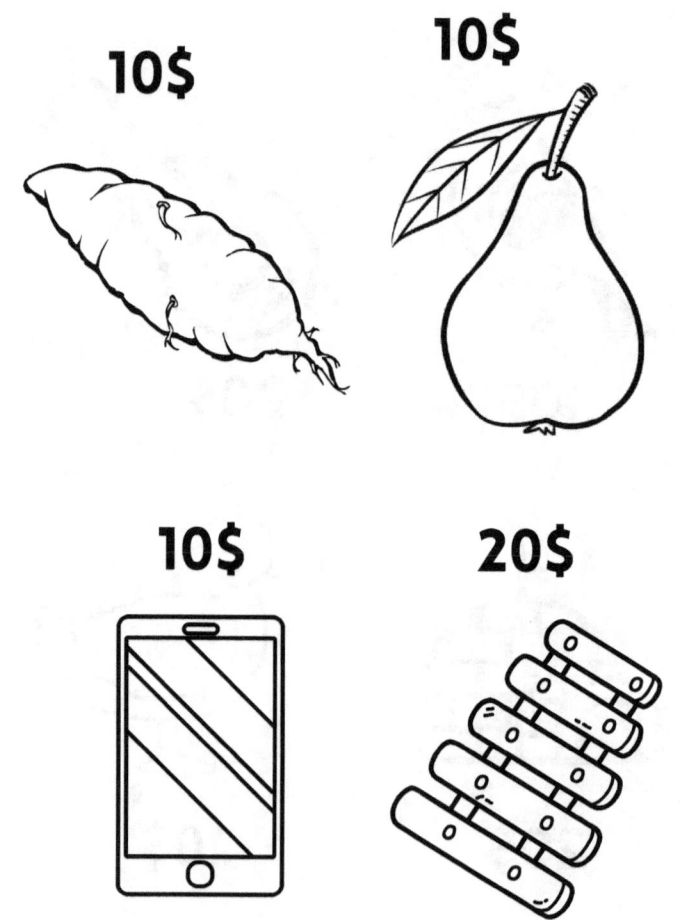

MINI LABYRINTHS

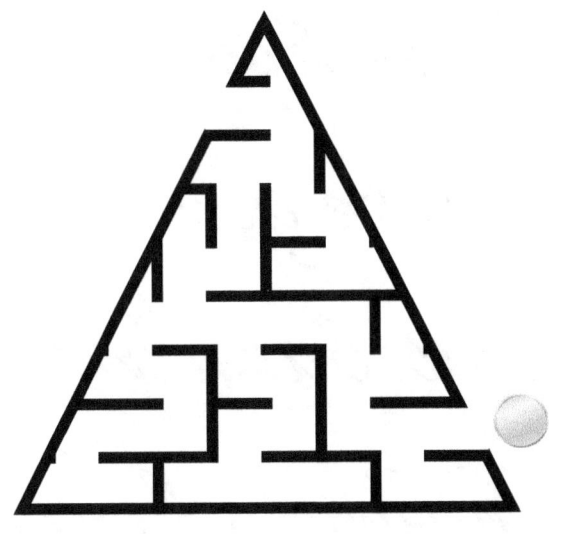

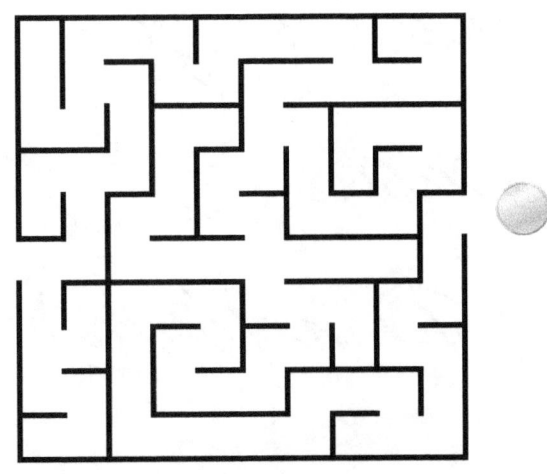

Save how and where you can, but never on love: when you love you waste.

(Don Tonio)

40$ IN ONE MONTH

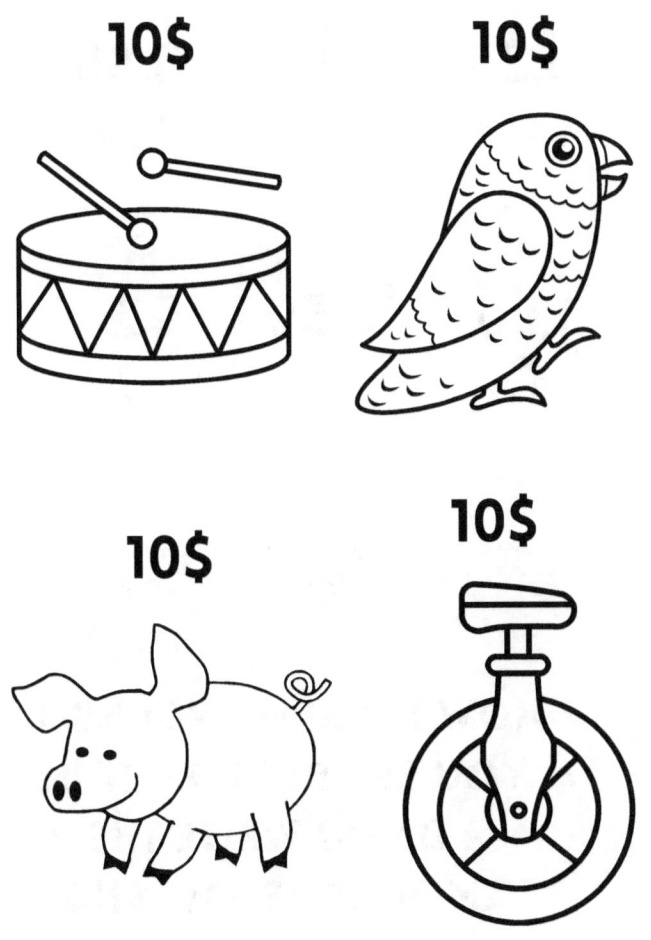

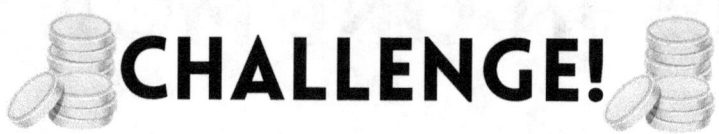
CHALLENGE!

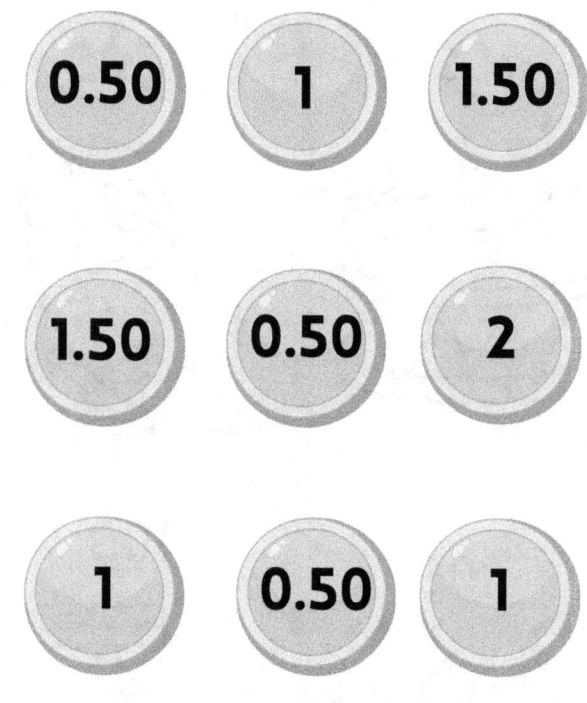

- HOW MUCH MONEY WILL YOU BE ABLE TO GET IN 4 DAYS? WRITE THE AMOUNT BELOW AND MARK WITH X

_____

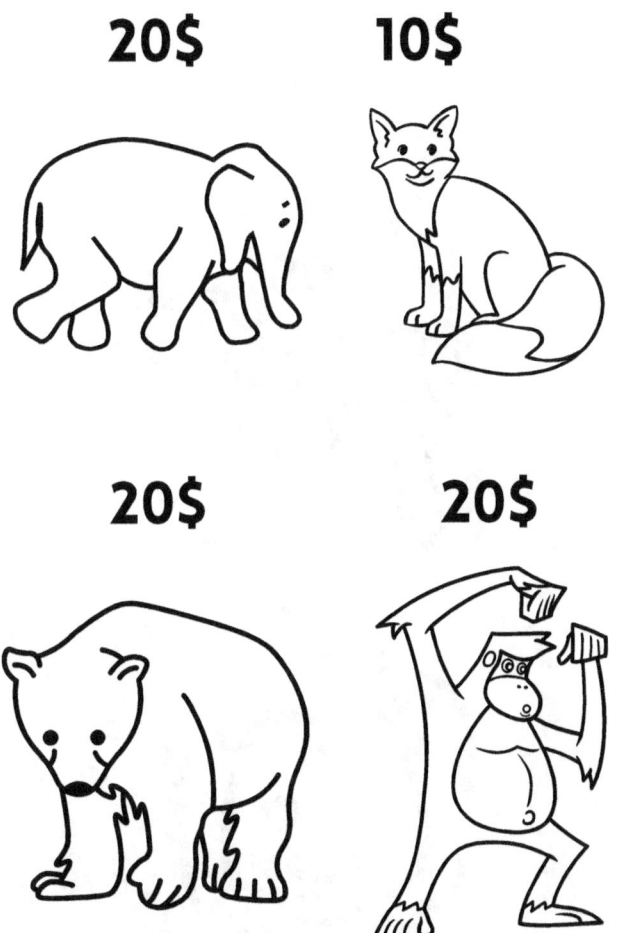

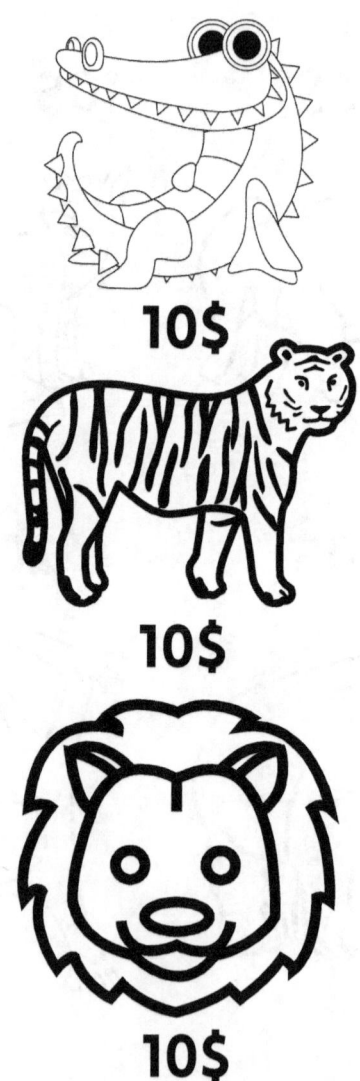

50$ IN ONE MONTH

10$ 20$

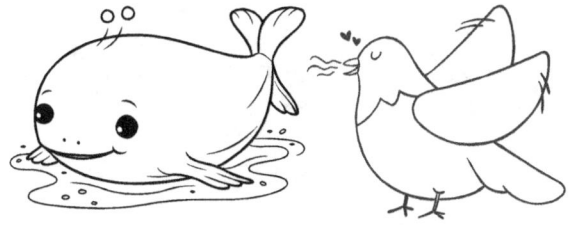

10$

10$

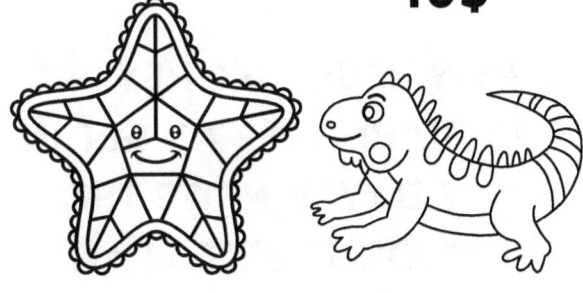

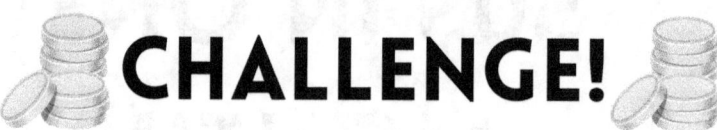

CHALLENGE!

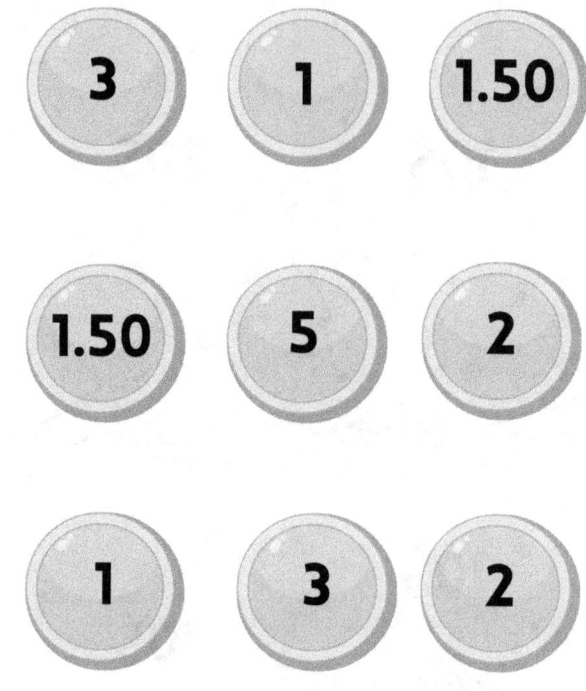

- HOW MUCH MONEY WILL YOU BE ABLE TO GET IN 7 DAYS? WRITE THE AMOUNT BELOW AND MARK WITH X

_____

60$ IN ONE MONTH

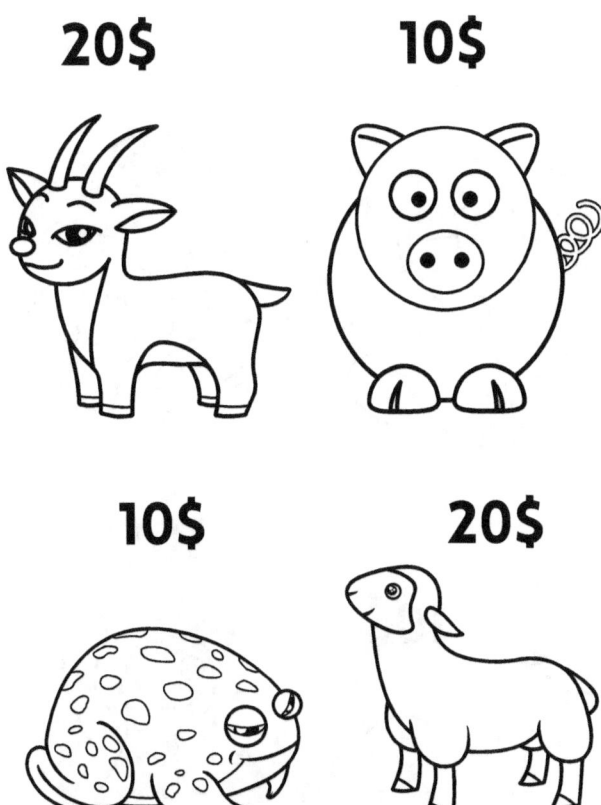

40$ IN ONE MONTH

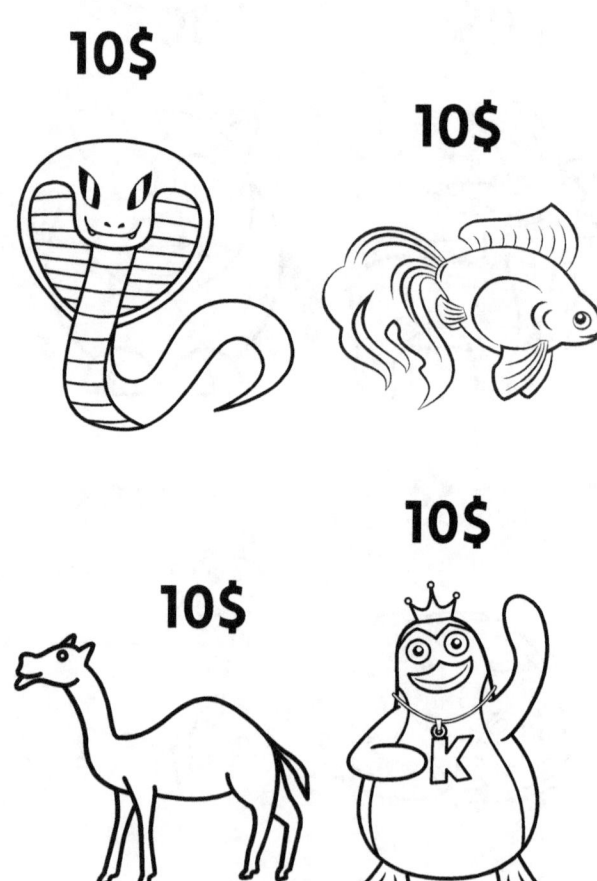

70$ IN ONE MONTH

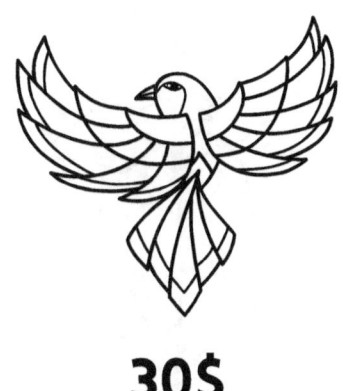

30$

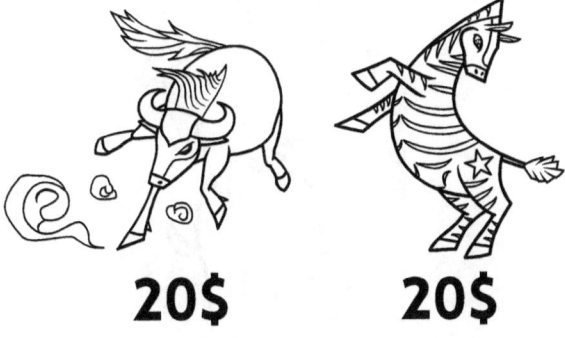

20$ 20$

35$ IN ONE MONTH

15$

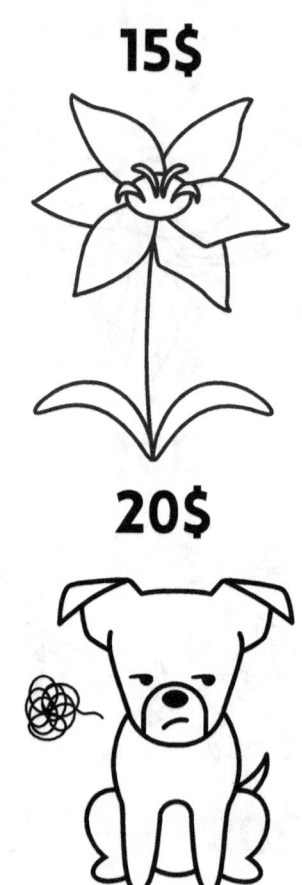

20$

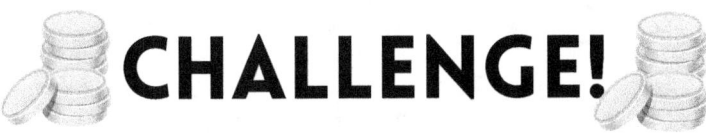
CHALLENGE!

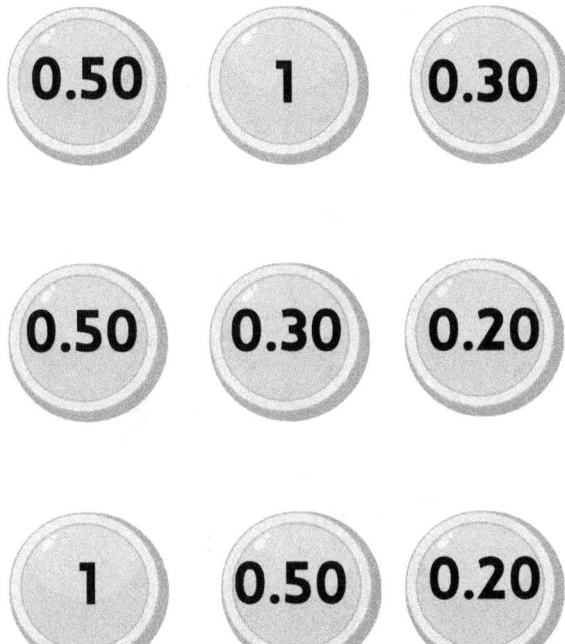

- HOW MUCH MONEY WILL YOU BE ABLE TO GET IN 2 DAYS? WRITE THE AMOUNT BELOW AND MARK WITH X

_____

50$ IN ONE MONTH

20$

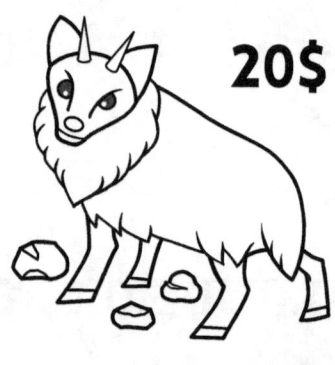

10$

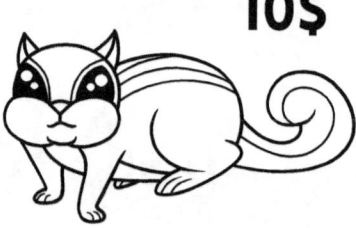

20$

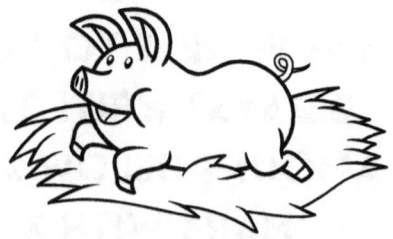

the path to wealth depends on two things: work and savings

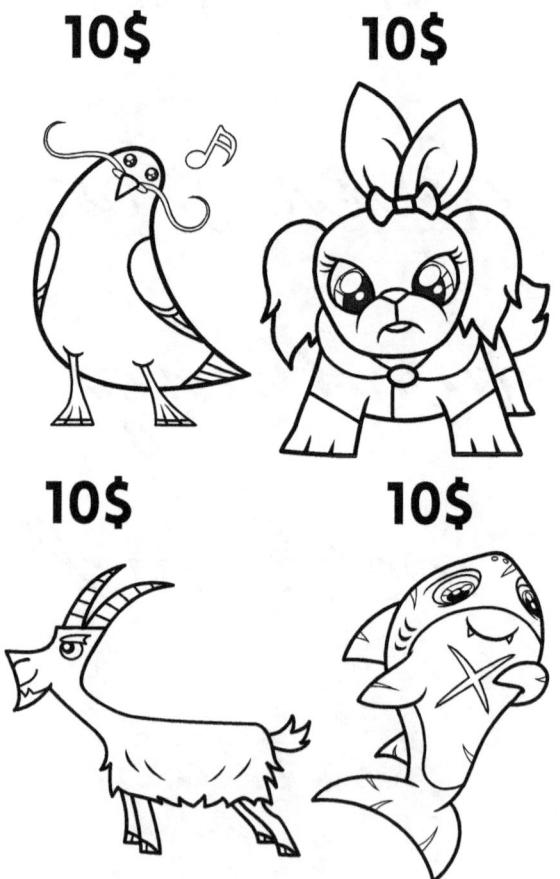

MINI LABYRINTHS

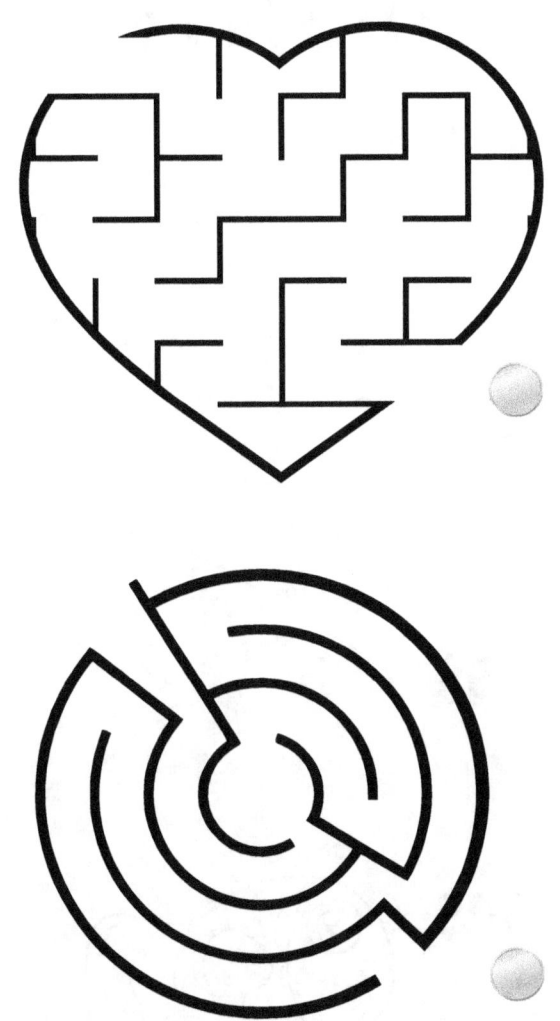

35$ IN ONE MONTH

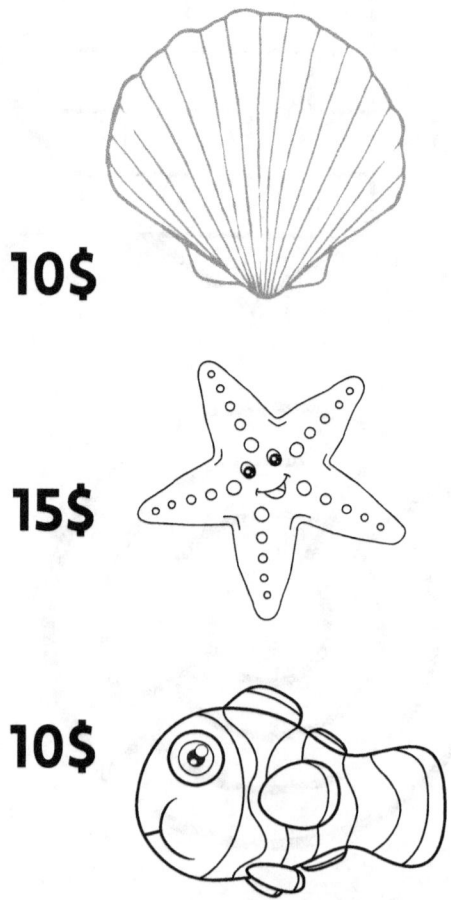

10$

15$

10$

70$ IN ONE MONTH

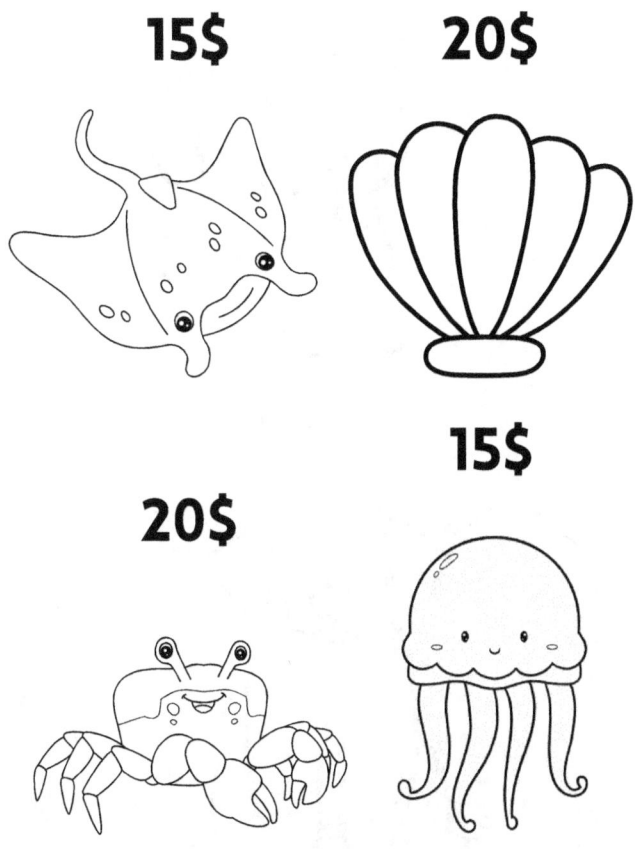

35$ IN ONE MONTH

15$

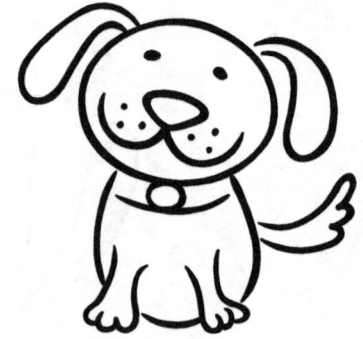

20$

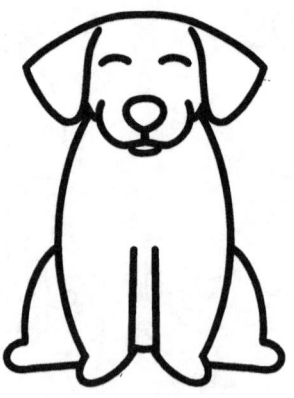

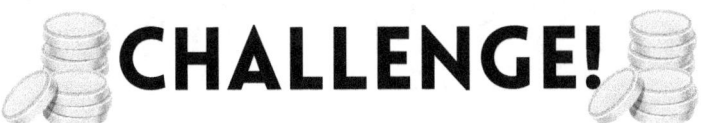

CHALLENGE!

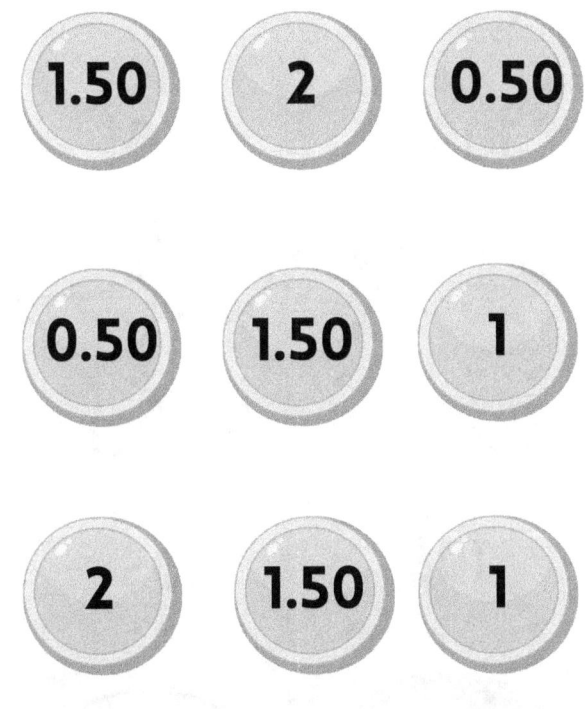

HOW MUCH MONEY WILL YOU BE ABLE TO GET IN 3 DAYS? WRITE THE AMOUNT BELOW AND MARK WITH X

_____

40$ IN ONE MONTH

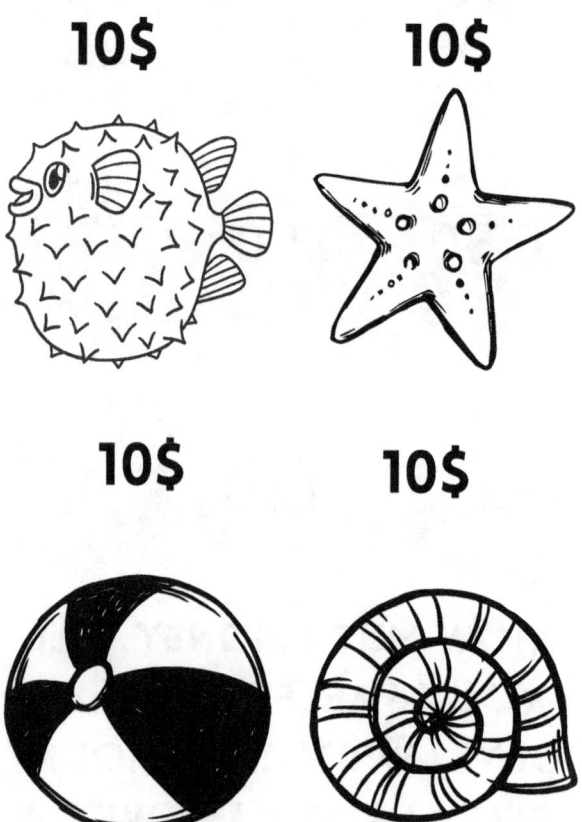

50$ IN ONE MONTH

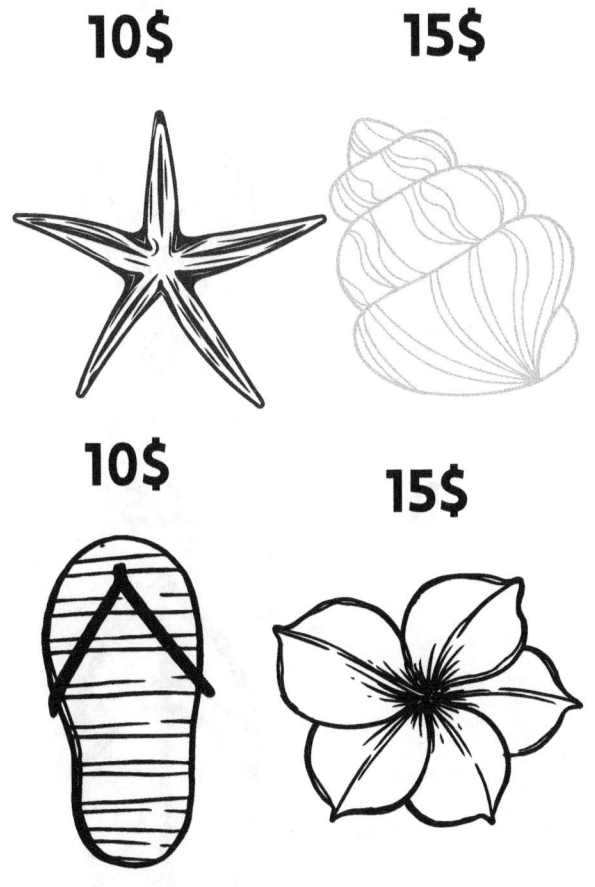

10$ 15$

10$ 15$

40$ IN ONE MONTH

10$**   **10$

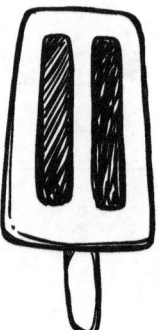 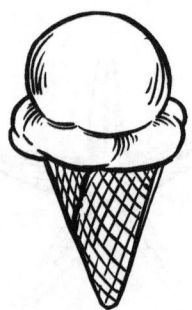

10$**   **10$

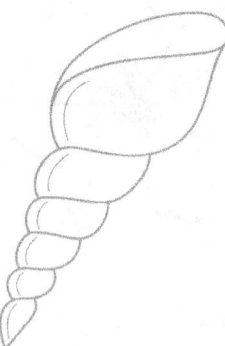 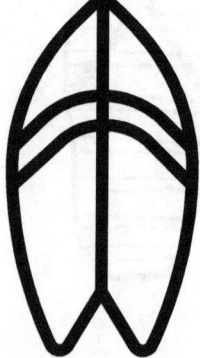

60$ IN ONE MONTH

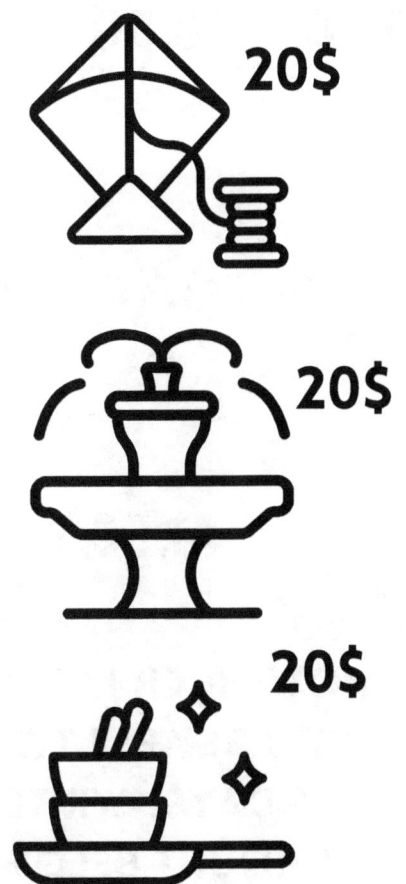

20$

20$

20$

CHALLENGE!

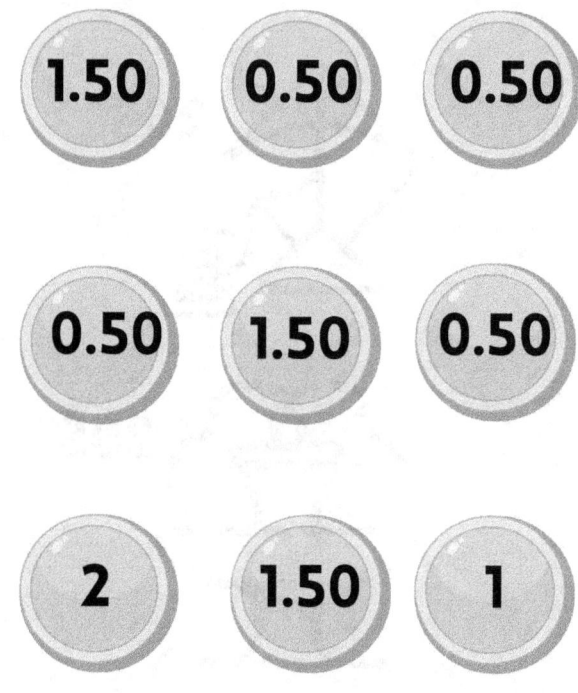

- HOW MUCH MONEY WILL YOU BE ABLE TO GET IN 4 DAYS? WRITE THE AMOUNT BELOW AND MARK WITH X

_____

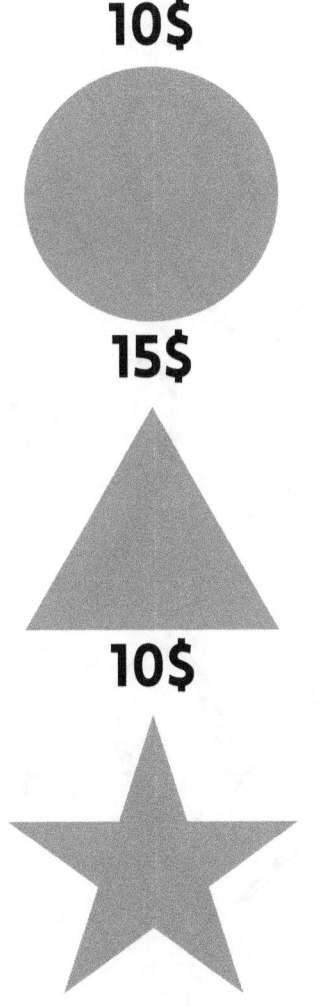

60$ IN ONE MONTH

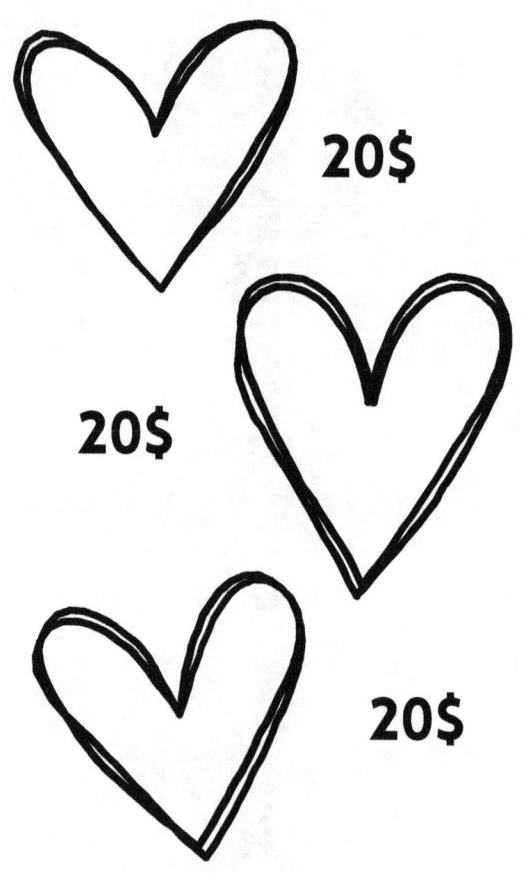

20$

20$

20$

40$ IN ONE MONTH

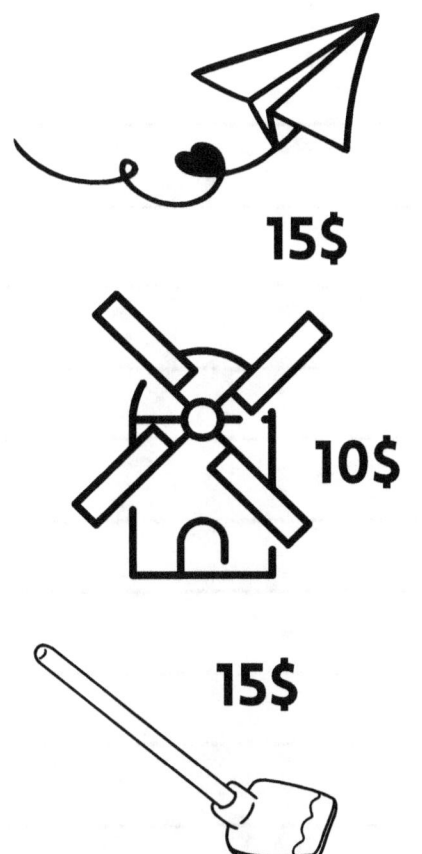

15$

10$

15$

DO YOU HAVE A NEW GOAL?

_____

_____

_____

_____

_____

_____

_____

_____

_____

"If you add a little to a little, but do so frequently, the little will soon become a lot."

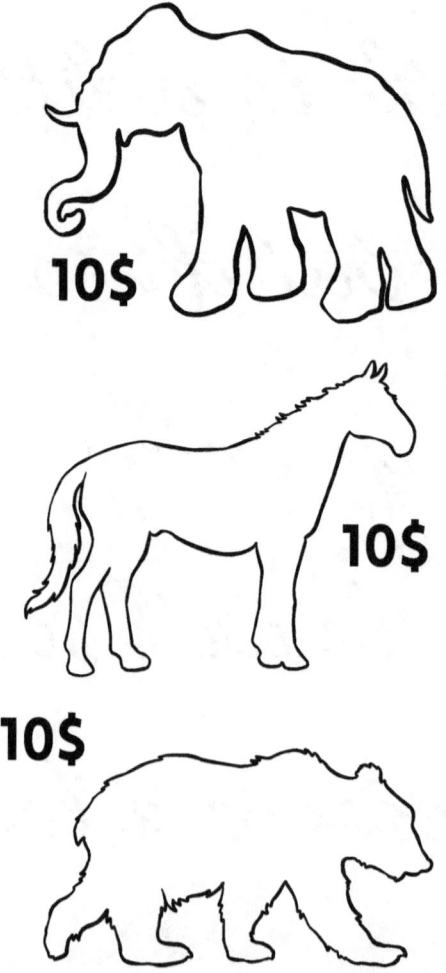

MINI LABYRINTHS

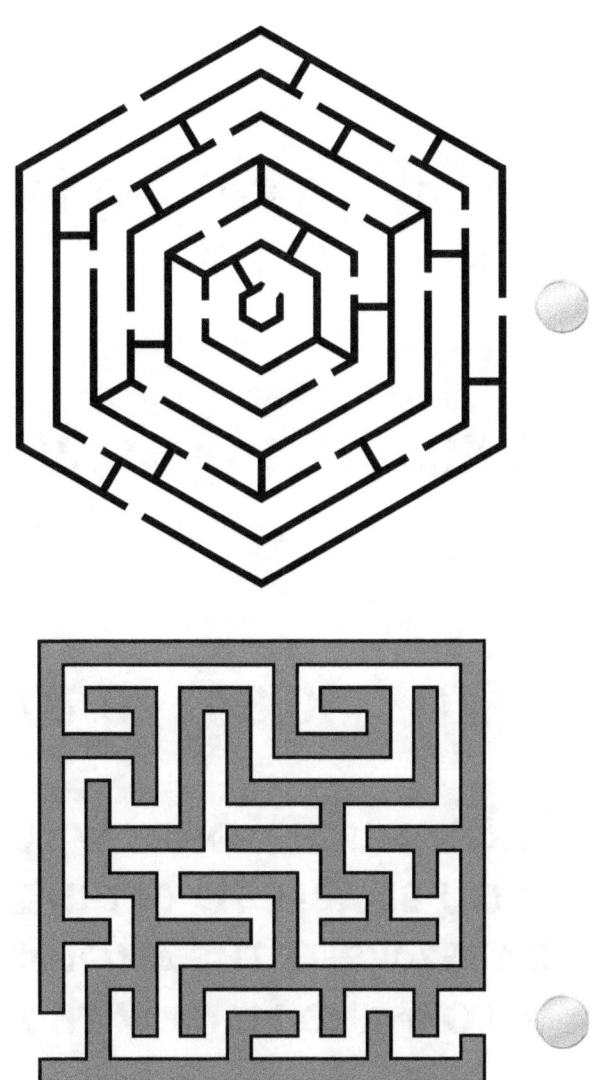

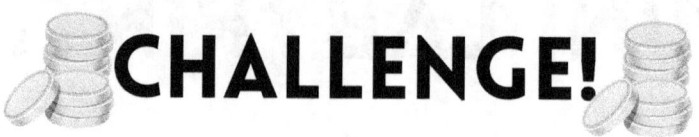 CHALLENGE!

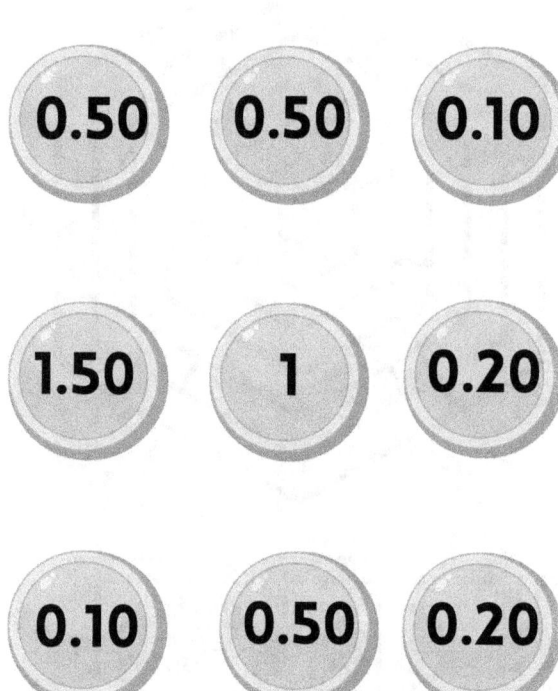

HOW MUCH MONEY WILL YOU BE ABLE TO GET IN 2 DAYS? WRITE THE AMOUNT BELOW AND MARK WITH X!

———

60$ IN ONE MONTH

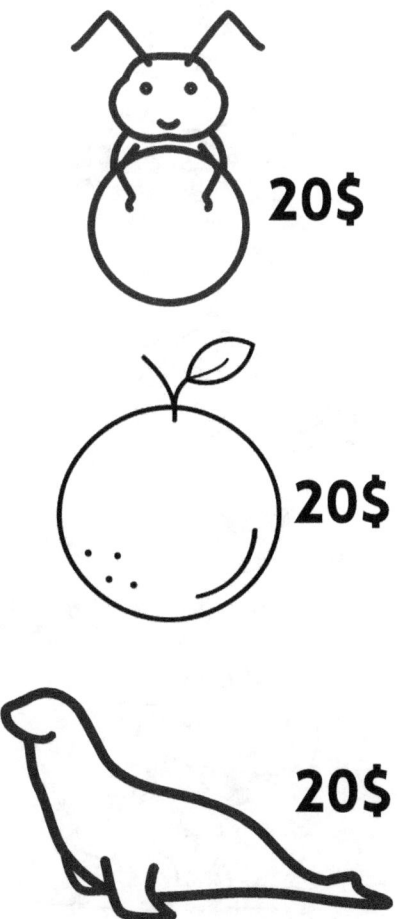

45$ IN ONE MONTH

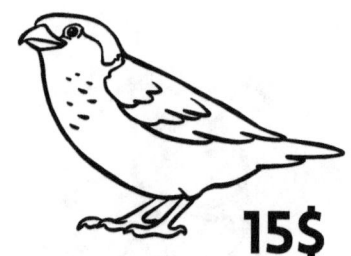

15$

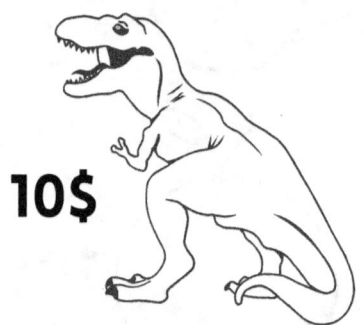

10$

15$

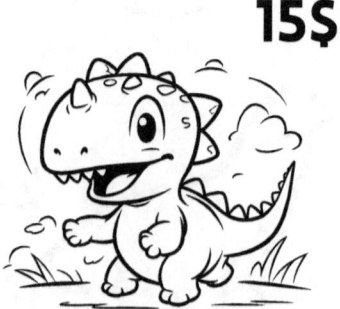

30$ IN ONE MONTH

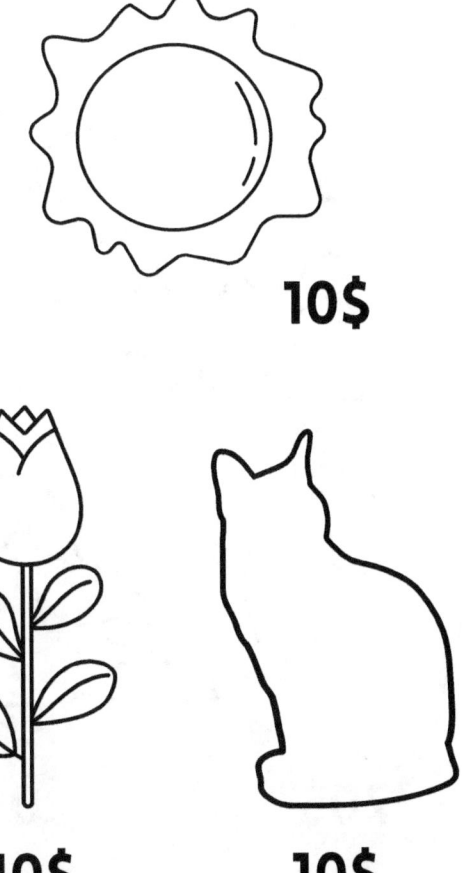

10$

10$ 10$

60$ IN ONE MONTH

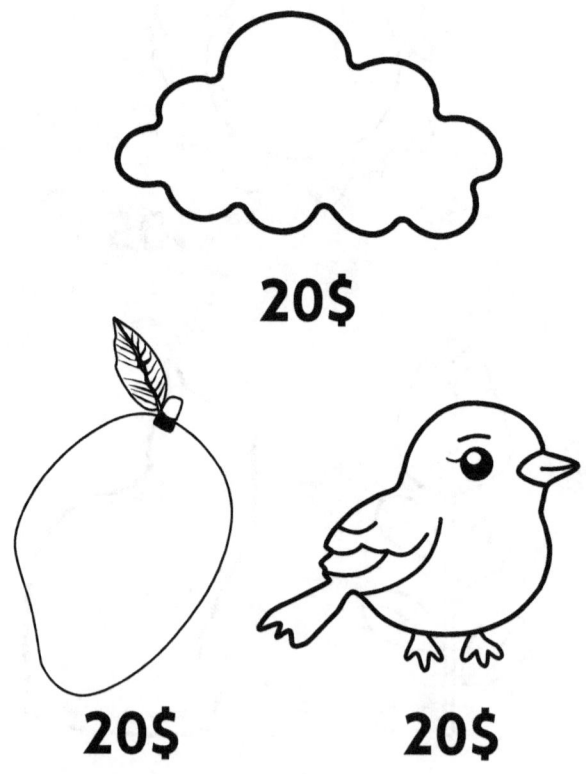

20$

20$ 20$

40$ IN ONE MONTH

10$ 10$

 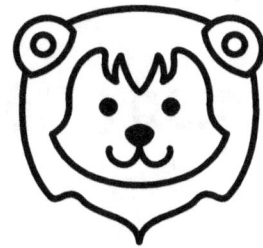

10$ 10$

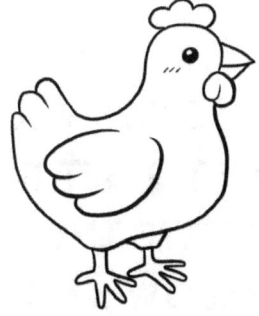 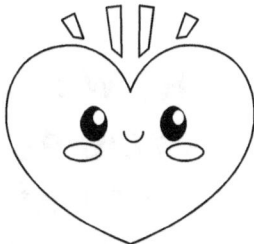

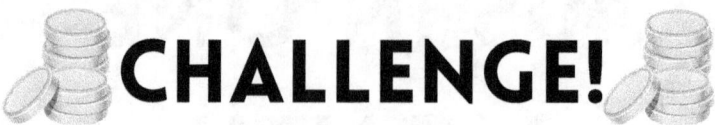
CHALLENGE!

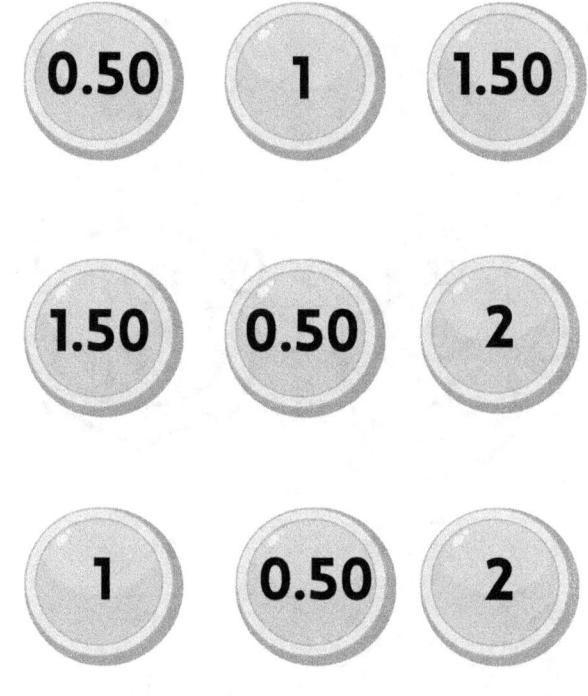

- HOW MUCH MONEY WILL YOU BE ABLE TO GET IN 3 DAYS? WRITE THE AMOUNT BELOW AND MARK WITH X!

_____

-

70$ IN ONE MONTH

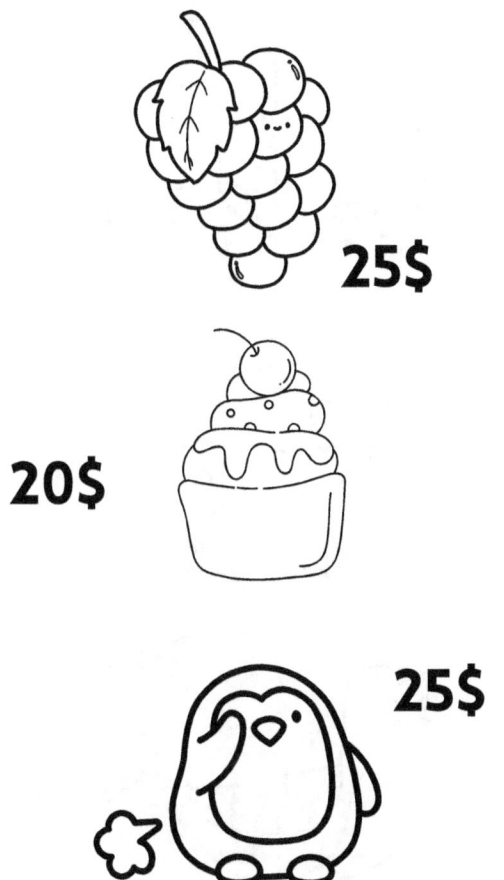

25$

20$

25$

35$ IN ONE MONTH

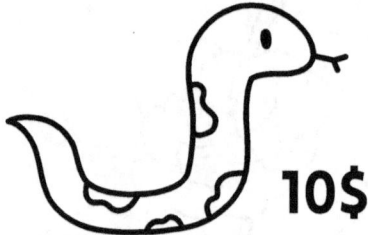 10$

15$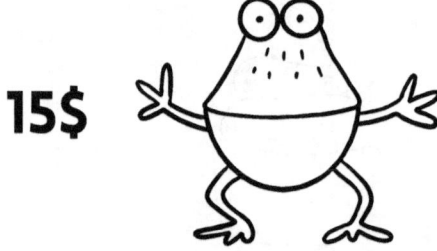

10$
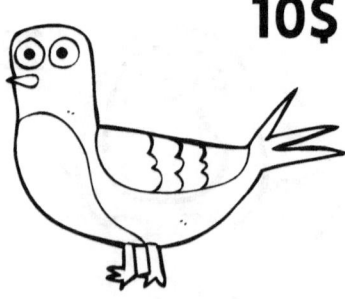

50$ IN ONE MONTH

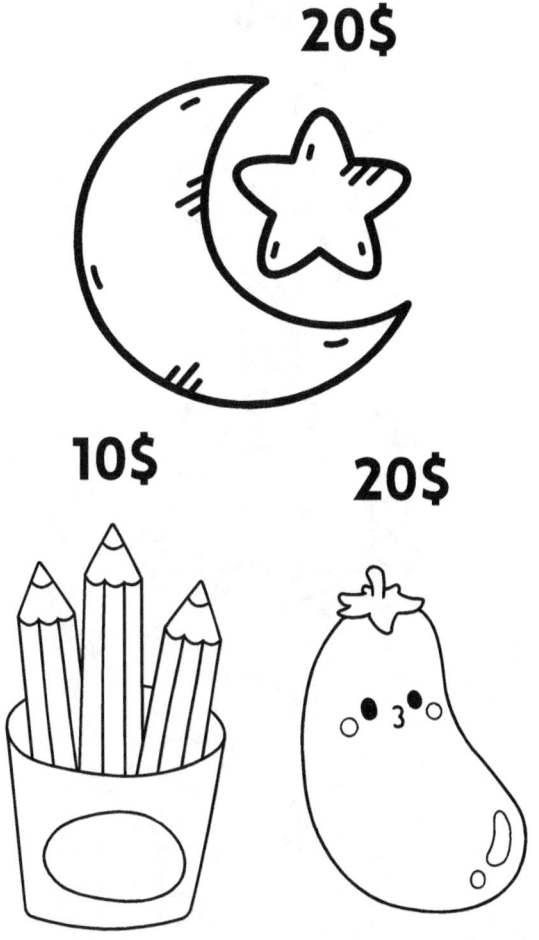

35$ IN ONE MONTH

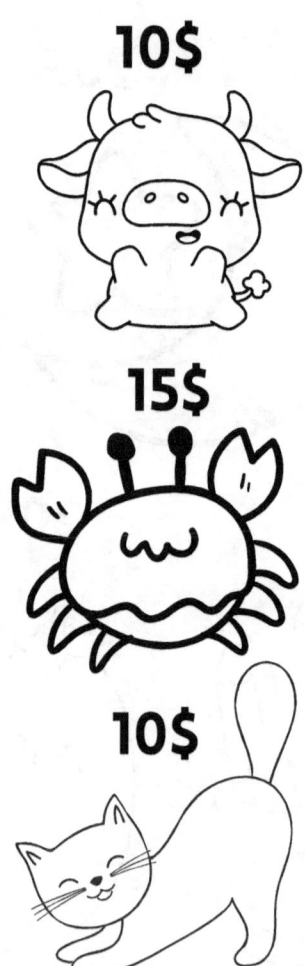

10$

15$

10$

60$ IN ONE MONTH

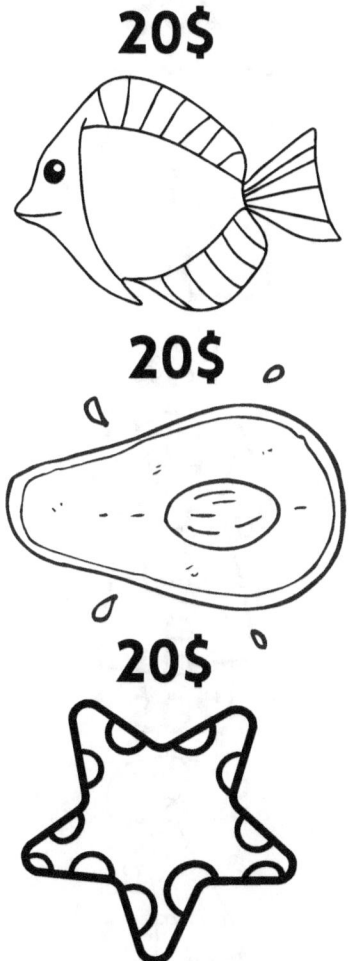

50$ IN ONE MONTH

20$

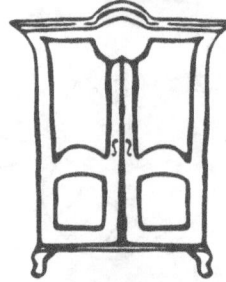

10$

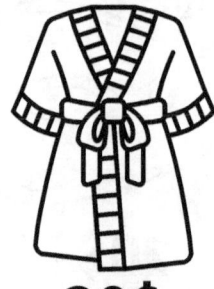

20$

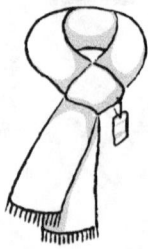

35$ IN ONE MONTH

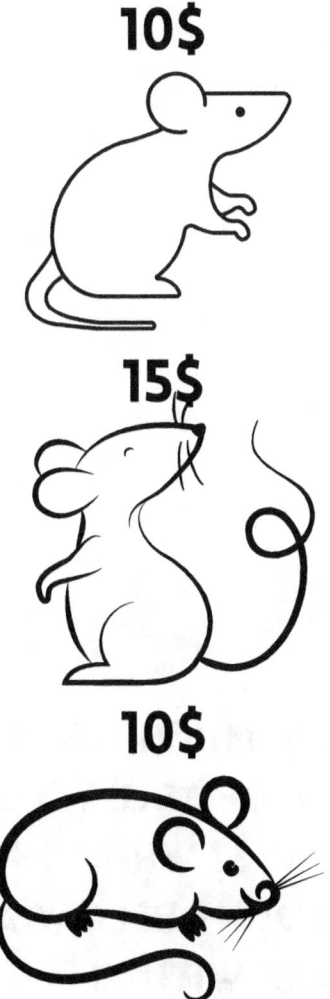

10$

15$

10$

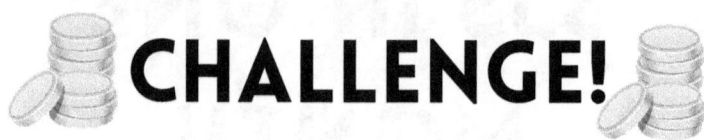

CHALLENGE!

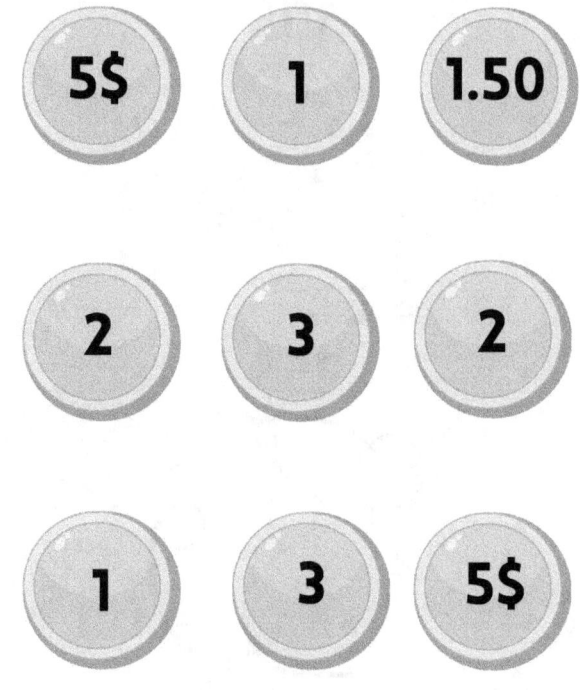

- HOW MUCH MONEY WILL YOU BE ABLE TO GET IN 7 DAYS? WRITE THE AMOUNT BELOW AND MARK WITH X!

_____

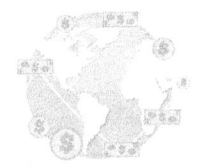

"Economy is about knowing how to spend and saving is about knowing how to maintain."

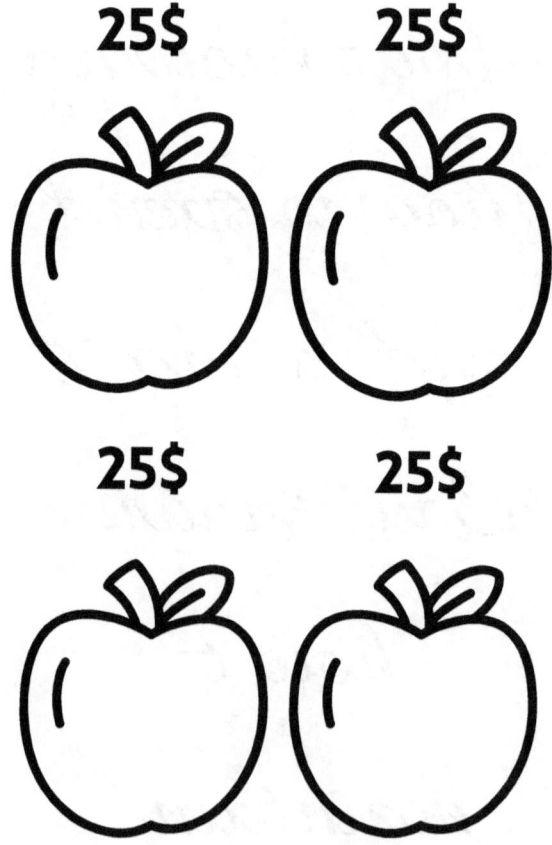

120$ IN ONE MONTH
HARD

30$ 30$

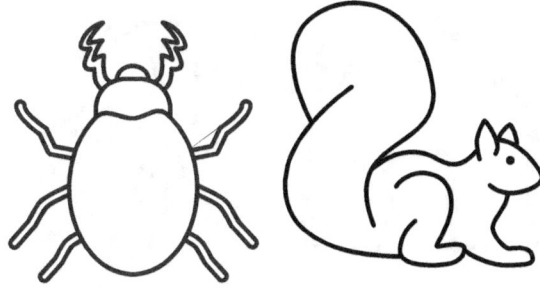

30$ 30$

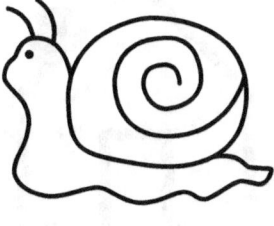 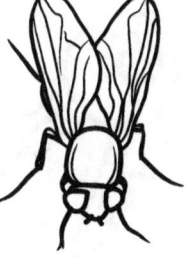

100$ IN ONE MONTH
HARD

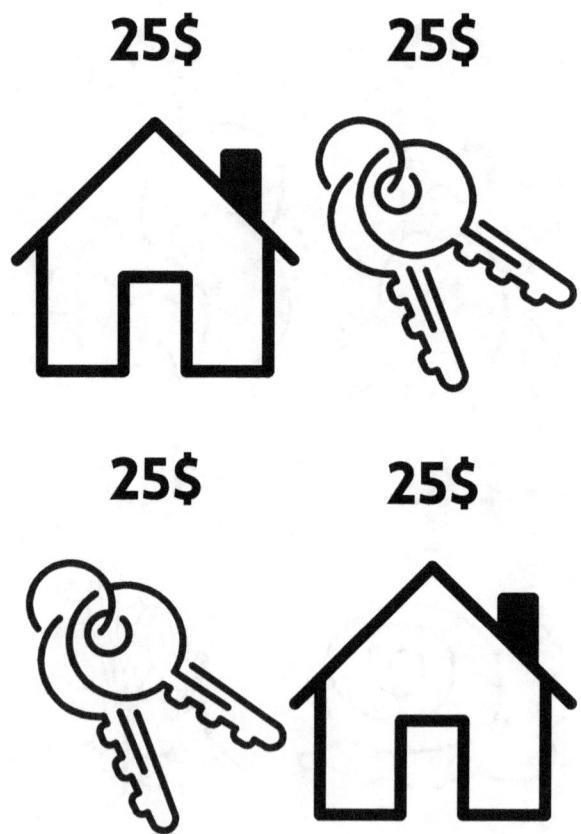

25$ 25$

25$ 25$

120$ IN ONE MONTH
HARD

30$ 30$

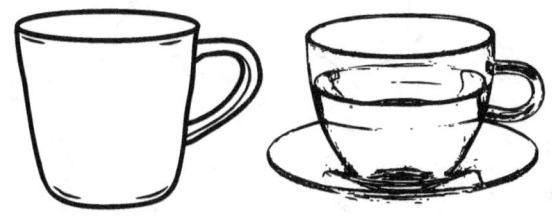

30$ 30$

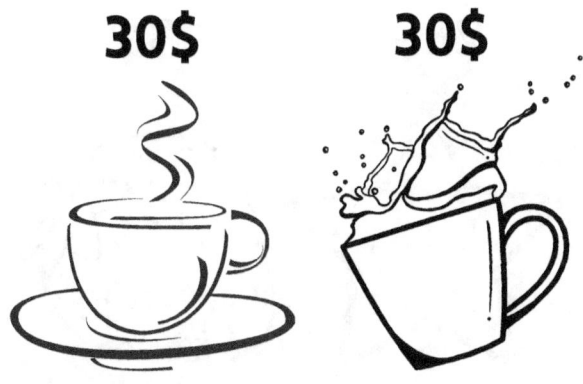

100$ IN ONE MONTH
HARD

25$ 25$

25$ 25$

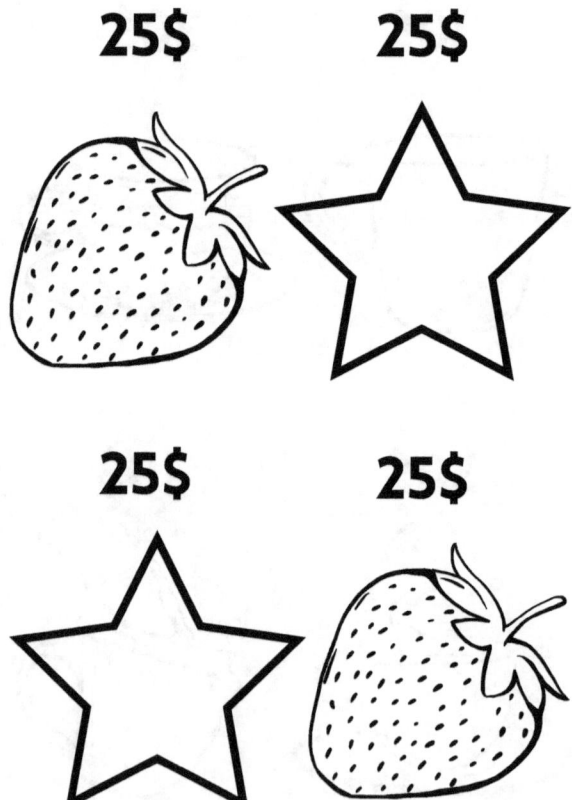

120$ IN ONE MONTH
HARD

30$ 30$

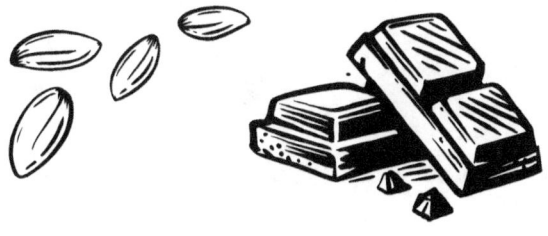

30$ 30$

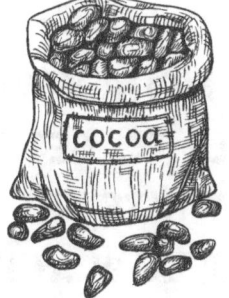
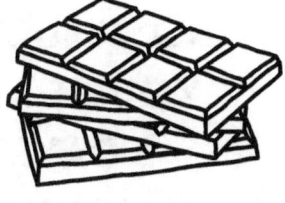

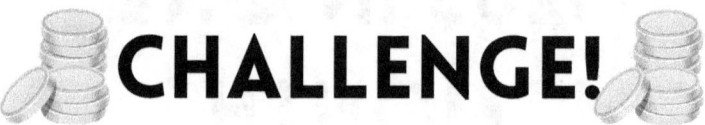
CHALLENGE!

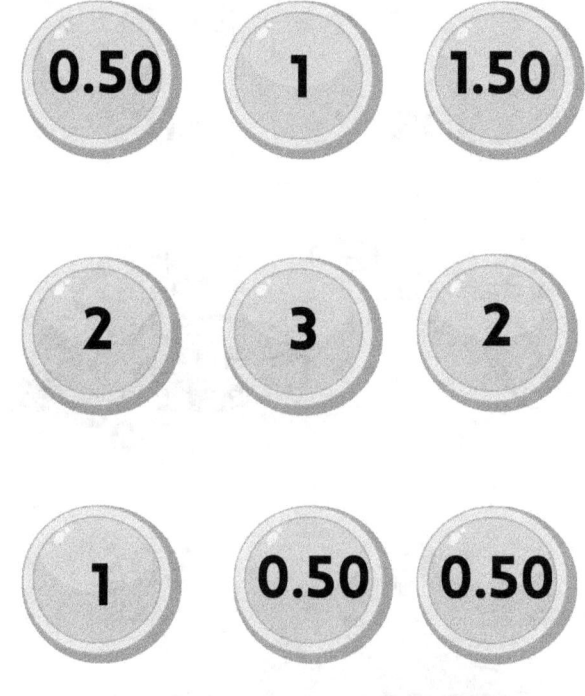

- HOW MUCH MONEY WILL YOU BE ABLE TO GET IN 5 DAYS? WRITE THE AMOUNT BELOW AND MARK WITH X!

_____

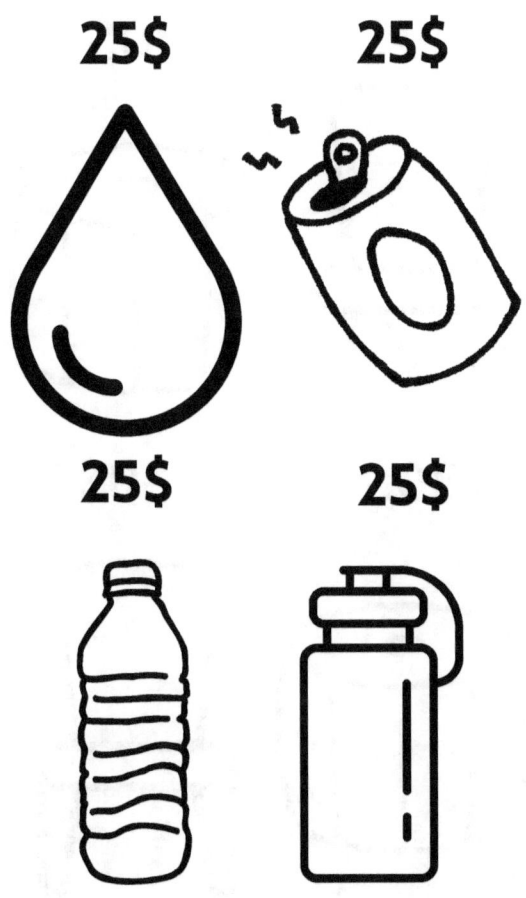

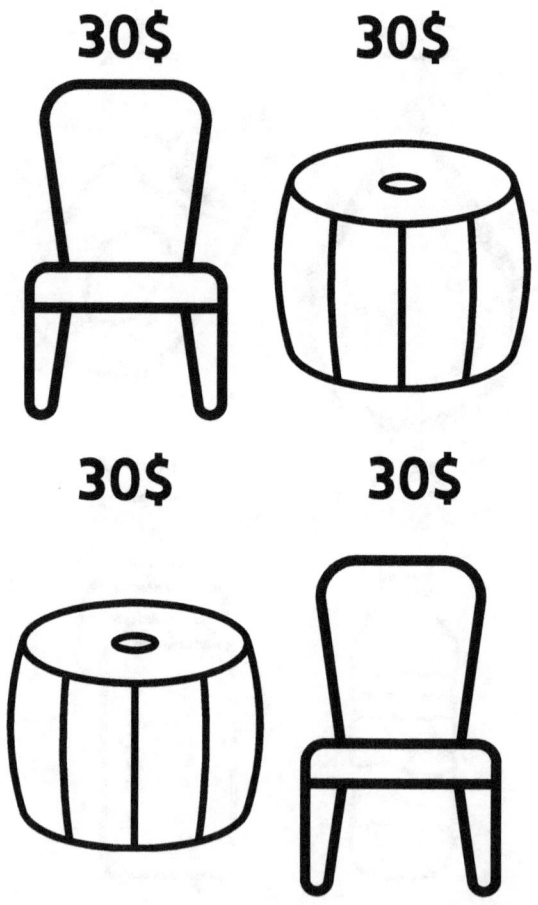

100$ IN ONE MONTH
HARD

25$ 25$

25$ 25$

150$ IN ONE MONTH
IMPOSSIBLE

25$ 50$

50$ 25$

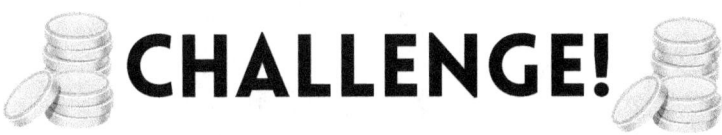

CHALLENGE!

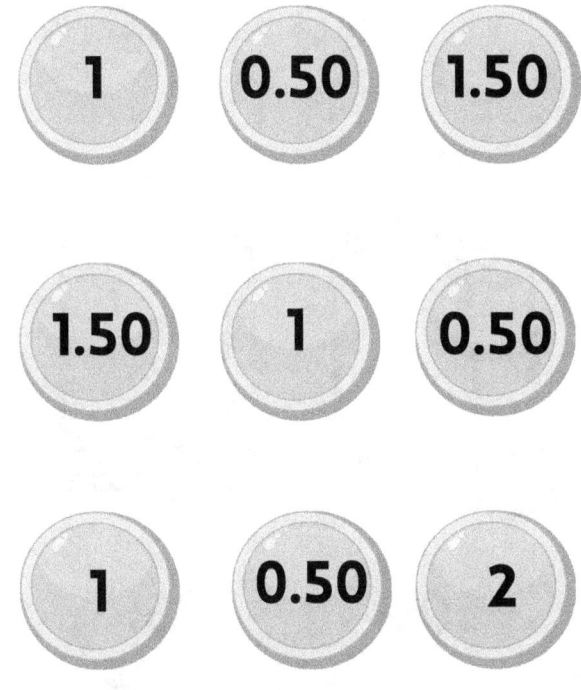

- HOW MUCH MONEY WILL YOU BE ABLE TO GET IN 4 DAYS? WRITE THE AMOUNT BELOW AND MARK WITH X!

_____

150$ IN ONE MONTH
IMPOSSIBLE

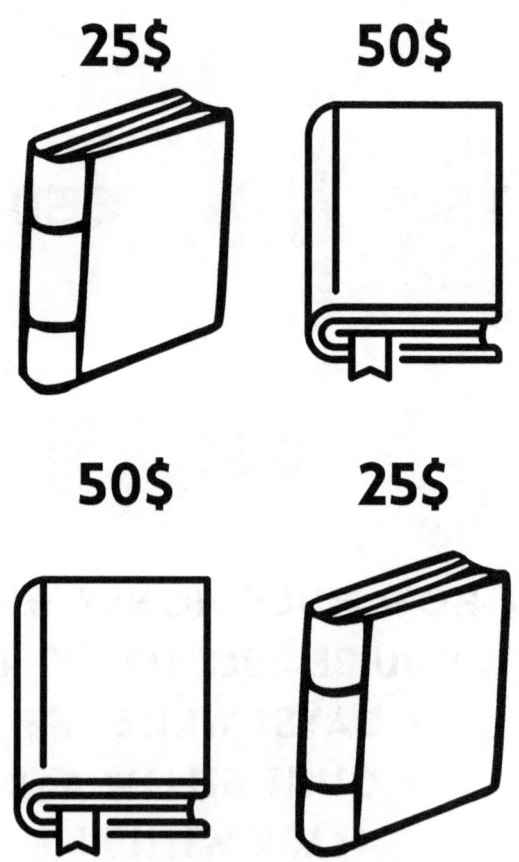

150$ IN ONE MONTH
IMPOSSIBLE

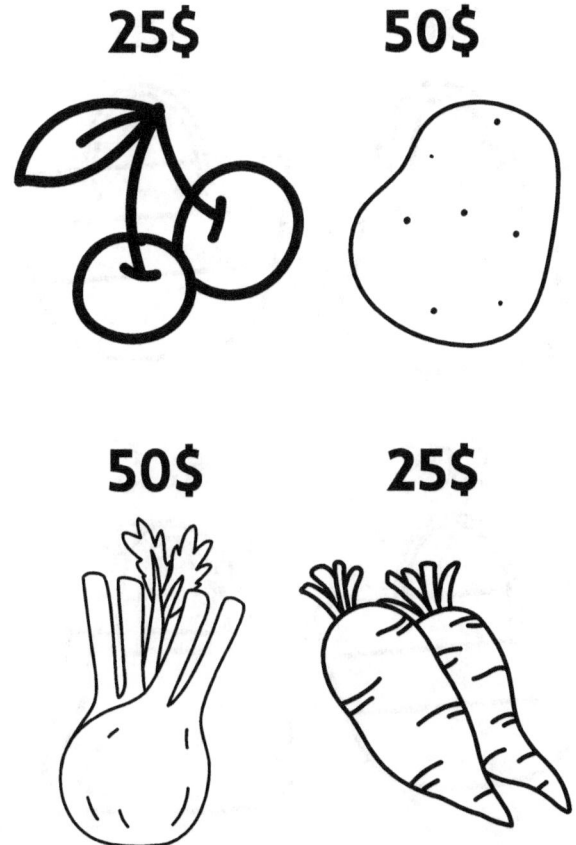

25$

50$

50$

25$

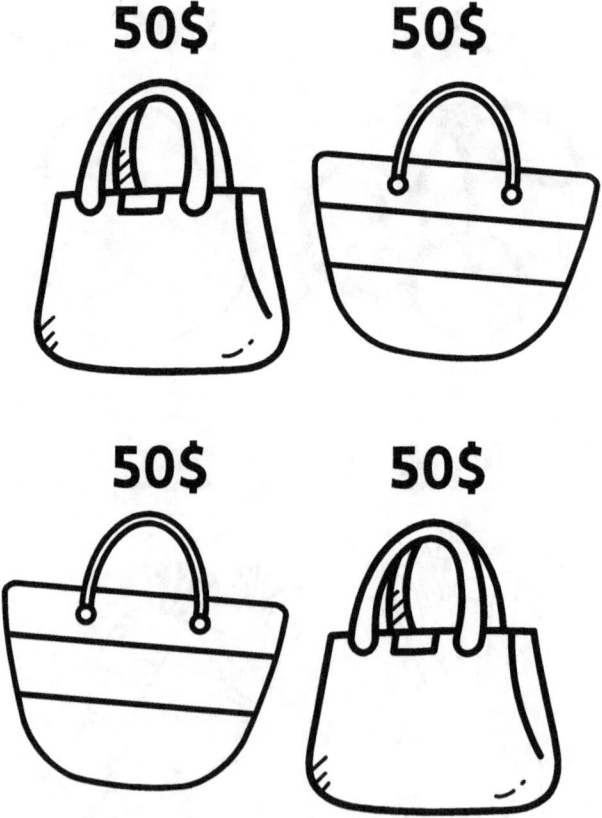

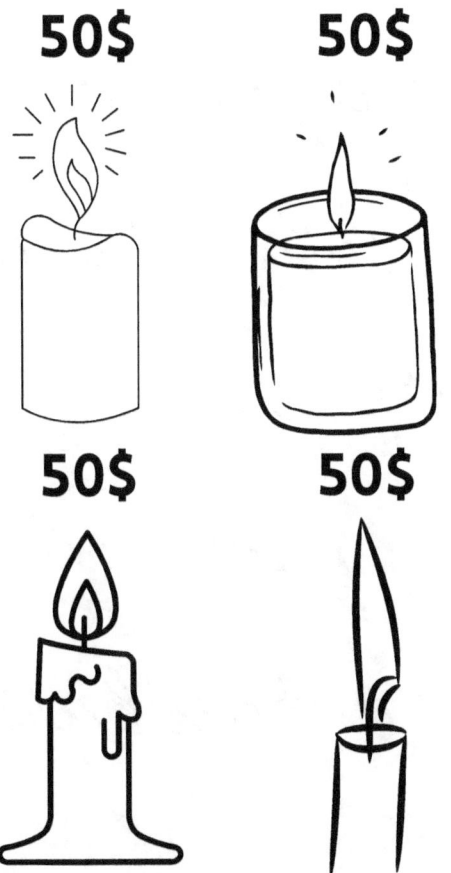

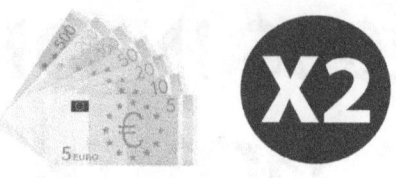

The surest way to double your money is to fold it in half and put it in your pocket.
(Kin Hubbard)

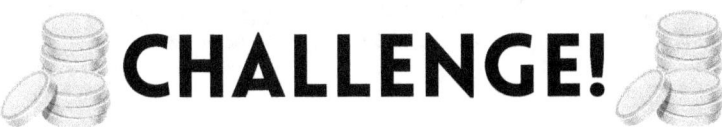
CHALLENGE!

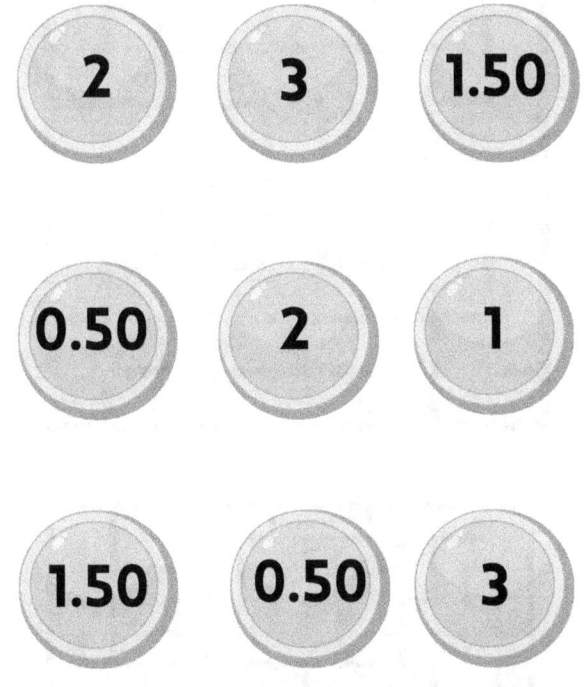

- HOW MUCH MONEY WILL YOU BE ABLE TO GET IN 5 DAYS? WRITE THE AMOUNT BELOW AND MARK WITH X!

_____

MINI LABYRINTHS

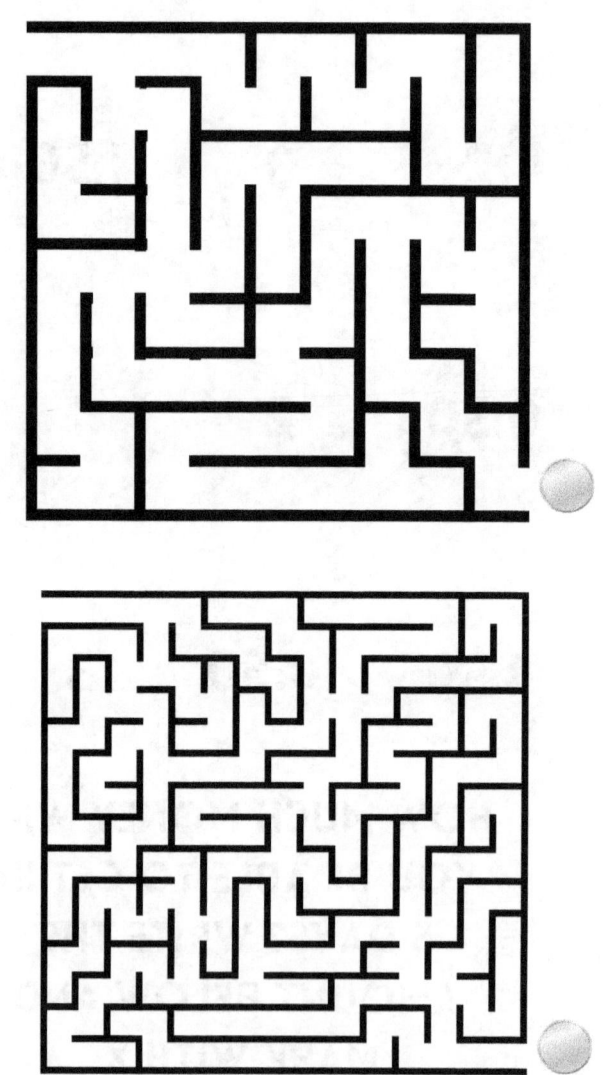

NOTES:

THANK YOU FOR CHOOSING ME!
I HOPE I HAVE HELPED YOU ACHIEVE YOUR GOALS OR MADE YOU EARN A NICE SUM ;)
LEAVE A NICE REVIEW!
<3

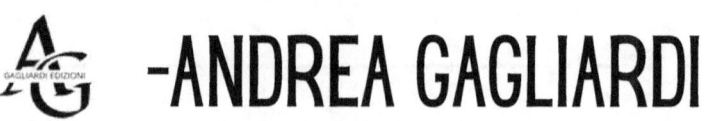 -ANDREA GAGLIARDI

www.ingramcontent.com/pod-product-compliance
Lightning Source LLC
Chambersburg PA
CBHW070317230526
45470CB00002B/921